A
BO
IR
V E

With Illustrations
from the National
Gallery of Ireland

CHRONICLE BOOKS

SAN FRANCISCO

CONTENTS

from PATRICK'S BREASTPLATE

Christ with me, Christ before me, Christ behind me,
Christ in me, Christ beneath me, Christ above me,
Christ on my right, Christ on my left,
Christ when I lie down, Christ when I sit down,
    Christ when I arise,
Christ in the heart of every man who thinks of me,
Christ in the mouth of every one who speaks of me,
Christ in every eye that sees me,
Christ in every ear that hears me.

Anon. (trans Kuno Meyer)

THE OLD WOMAN

As a white candle
In a holy place,
So is the beauty
Of an aged face.

As the spent radiance
Of the winter sun,
So is a woman
With her travail done.

Her brood gone from her,
And her thoughts as still
As the waters
Under a ruined mill.

Joseph Campbell
(1879-1944)

'ICHAM OF IRLAUNDE'

Icham of Irlaunde
Ant of the holy londe of irlonde
Gode sir pray ich ye
for of saynte charite,
come ant daunce wyt me,
in irlaunde.

Anon.

THE LAKE ISLE OF INNISFREE

I will arise and go now, and go to Innisfree,
And a small cabin build there, of clay and wattles
     made:
Nine bean-rows will I have there, a hive for the
     honey-bee,
And live alone in the bee-loud glade.

And I shall have some peace there, for peace comes
     dropping slow,
Dropping from the veils of the morning to where the
     cricket sings;
There midnight's all a glimmer, and noon a purple
     glow,
And evening full of the linnet's wings.

I will arise and go now, for always night and day
I hear lake water lapping with low sounds by the
     shore;
While I stand on the roadway, or on the pavement
     grey,
I hear it in the deep heart's core.

W. B. Yeats
(1865-1939)

ON STELLA'S BIRTHDAY

Stella this day is thirty-four
(We shan't dispute a year or more),
However Stella, be not troubled,
Although thy size and years are doubled,
Since first I saw thee at sixteen
The brightest virgin on the green,
So little is thy form declin'd
Made up so largely in thy mind.
Oh, would it please the gods to split
Thy beauty, size, and years, and wit,
No age could furnish out a pair
Of nymphs so graceful, wise and fair
With half the lustre of your eyes,
With half your wit, your years and size:
And then before it grew too late,
How should I beg of gentle Fate
(That either nymph might have her swain)
To split my worship too in twain.

Jonathan Swift
(1667-1745)

'THE HARP THAT ONCE THROUGH TARA'S HALLS'

The harp that once through Tara's halls
The soul of music shed,
Now hangs as mute on Tara's walls
As if that soul were fled.
So sleeps the pride of former days,
So glory's thrill is o'er,
And hearts that once beat high for praise,
Now feel that pulse no more!

No more to chiefs and ladies bright
The harp of Tara swells;
The chord alone that breaks at night,
Its tale of ruin tells.
Thus Freedom now so seldom wakes,
The only throb she gives
Is when some heart indignant breaks,
To show that still she lives.

Thomas Moore
(1779-1852)

DEAR BLACK HEAD

Put your head, darling, darling, darling,
Your darling black head my heart above;
Oh, mouth of honey, with the thyme for fragrance,
Who, with heart in breast, could deny you love?

Oh, many and many a young girl for me is pining,
Letting her locks of gold to the cold wind free,
For me, the foremost of our gay young fellows;
But I'd leave a hundred, pure love, for thee!

Then put your head, darling, darling, darling,
Your darling black head my heart above;
Oh, mouth of honey, with the thyme for fragrance,
Who, with heart in breast, could deny you love?

Anon. (trans Samuel Ferguson)

The Stars Stand up in the Air

The stars stand up in the air
The sun and the moon are gone,
The strand of its waters is bare,
And her sway is swept from the swan.

The cuckoo was calling all day,
Hid in the branches above,
How my stórín is fled away,
'Tis my grief that I gave her my love!

Three things through love I see –
Sorrow and sin and death –
And my mind reminding me
That this doom I breathe with my breath.

But sweeter than violin or lute
Is my love – and she left me behind.
I wish that all music were mute,
And I to all beauty were blind.

She's more shapely than swan by the strand,
She's more radiant than grass after dew,
She's more fair than the stars where they stand –
'Tis my grief that her ever I knew!

Anon. (trans Thomas MacDonagh)

HE BIDS HIS BELOVED BE AT PEACE

I hear the Shadowy Horses, their long manes a-shake,
Their hoofs heavy with tumult, their eyes glimmering
    white;
The North unfolds above them clinging, creeping
    night,
The East her hidden joy before the morning break,
The West weeps in pale dew and sighs passing away,
The South is pouring down roses of crimson fire:
O vanity of Sleep, Hope, Dream, endless Desire,
The Horses of Disaster plunge in the heavy clay:
Beloved, let your eyes half close, and your heart beat
Over my heart, and your hair fall over my breast,
Drowning love's lonely hour in deep twilight of rest,
And hiding their tossing manes and their tumultuous
    feet.

W. B. Yeats
(1865-1939)

ON HIS OWN DEAFNESS

Deaf, giddy, helpless, left alone,
To all my Friends a Burthen grown,
No more I hear my Chuch's Bell,
Than if it rang out for my Knell:
At Thunder now no more I start,
Than at the Rumbling of a Cart:
Nay, what's incredible, alack!
I hardly hear a Woman's Clack.

Jonathan Swift
(1667-1745)

I See his Blood upon the Rose

I see his blood upon the rose
And in the stars the glory of his eyes,
His body gleams amid eternal snows,
His tears fall from the skies.

I see his face in every flower;
The thunder and the singing of the birds
Are but his voice – and carven by his power
Rocks are his written words.

All pathways by his feet are worn,
His strong heart stirs the ever-beating sea,
His crown of thorns is twined with every thorn,
His cross is every tree.

Joseph Plunkett
(1887-1916)

Adieu to evening dances, when merry neighbours
    meet,
And the fiddle says to boys and girls, 'Get up and
    shake your feet!'
To 'shanachus' and wise old talk of Erin's days gone
    by–
Who trench'd the rath on such a hill, and where the
    bones may lie
Of saint, or king, or warrier chief; with tales of fairy
    power,
And tender ditties sweetly sung to pass the twilight
    hour.
The mournful song of exile is now for me to learn–
Adieu, my dear companions on the winding banks
    of Erne!

William Allingham
(1824-1889)

''Tis the Last Rose of Summer'

'Tis the last rose of summer
Left blooming alone;
All her lovely companions
Are faded and gone;
No flower of her kindred,
No rose-bud is nigh,
To reflect back her blushes,
To give sigh for sigh.

I'll not leave thee, thou lone one!
To pine on the stem;
Since the lovely are sleeping,
Go sleep thou with them.
Thus kindly I scatter
Thy leaves o'er the bed,
Where thy mates of the garden
Lie scentless and dead.

So soon may *I* follow
When friendships decay,
And from Love's shining circle
The gems drop away.
When true hearts lie wither'd
And fond ones are flown,
Oh! who would inhabit
This bleak world alone?

Thomas Moore
(1779-1852)

JUNE

Broom out the floor now, lay the fender by,
And plant this bee-sucked bough of woodbine there,
And let the window down. The butterfly
Floats in upon the sunbeam, and the fair
Tanned face of June, the nomad gipsy, laughs
Above her widespread wares, the while she tells
The farmers' fortunes in the fields, and quaffs
The water from the spider-peopled wells.

The hedges are all drowned in green grass seas,
And bobbing poppies flare like Elmo's light,
While siren-like the pollen-stained bees
Drone in the clover depths. And up the height
The cuckoo's voice is hoarse and broke with joy.
And on the lowland crops the crows make raid,
Nor fear the clappers of the farmer's boy,
Who sleeps, like drunken Noah, in the shade.

And loop this red rose in that hazel ring
That snares your little ear, for June is short
And we must joy in it and dance and sing,
And from her bounty draw her rosy worth.
Ay! soon the swallows will be flying south,
The wind wheel north to gather in the snow,
Even the roses spilt on youth's red mouth
Will soon blow down the road all roses go.

Francis Ledwidge
(1891-1917)

BEFORE THE WORLD WAS MADE

If I make the lashes dark
And the eyes more bright
And the lips more scarlet,
Or ask if all be right
From mirror after mirror,
No vanity's displayed:
I'm looking for the face I had
Before the world was made.

What if I look upon a man
As though on my beloved,
And my blood be cold the while
And my heart unmoved?
Why should he think me cruel
Or that he is betrayed?
I'd have him love the thing that was
Before the world was made.

W. B. Yeats
(1865-1939)

Rest Only in the Grave

I rode till I reached the House of Wealth –
'Twas filled with riot and blighted health.

I rode till I reached the House of Love –
'Twas vocal with sighs beneath and above!

I rode till I reached the House of Sin –
There were shrieks and curses without and within.

I rode till I reached the House of Toil –
Its inmates had nothing to bake or boil.

I rode in search of the House of Content
But never could reach it, far as I went!

The House of Quiet, for strong and weak
And poor and rich, I have still to seek –

That House is narrow, and dark, and small
But the only Peaceful House of all.

James Clarence Mangan
(1803-1849)

from THE BALLAD OF READING GAOL

At last the dead man walked no more
Amongst the Trial Men,
And I knew that he was standing up
In the black dock's dreadful pen,
And that never would I see his face
For weal or woe again.

Like two doomed ships that pass in storm
We had crossed each other's way:
But we made no sign, we said no word,
We had no word to say;
For we did not meet in the holy night,
But in the shameful day.

A prison wall was round us both,
Two outcast men we were:
The world had thrust us from its heart,
And God from out His care:
And the iron gin that waits for Sin
Had caught us in its snare.

Oscar Wilde
(1854-1900)

Exiles

The gods have taken alien shapes upon them
Wild peasants driving swine
In a strange country. Through the swarthy faces
The starry faces shine.

Under grey tattered skies they strain and reel there:
Yet cannot all disguise
The majesty of fallen gods, the beauty,
The fire beneath their eyes.

They huddle at night within low clay-built cabins;
And, to themselves unknown,
They carry with them diadem and sceptre
And move from throne to throne.

George Russell (AE)
(1867-1935)

My Hope, My Love

My hope, my love, we will go
Into the woods, scattering the dews,
Where we will behold the salmon, and the ousel in its
    nest,
The deer and the roe-buck calling,
The sweetest bird on the branches warbling,
The cuckoo on the summit of the green hill;
And death shall never approach us
In the bosom of the fragrant wood!

Anon. (trans Edward Walsh)

THE BLACKBIRDS

I heard the Poor Old Woman say:
'At break of day the fowler came,
And took my blackbirds from their songs
Who loved me well thro' shame and blame.

No more from lovely distances
Their songs shall bless me mile by mile,
Nor to white Ashbourne call me down
To wear my crown another while.

With bended flowers the angels mark
For the skylark the place they lie,
From there its little family
Shall dip their wings first in the sky.

And when the first surprise of flight
Sweet songs excite, from the far dawn
Shall there come blackbirds loud with love,
Sweet echoes of the singers gone.

But in the lonely hush of eve
Weeping I grieve the silent bills.'
I heard the Poor Old Woman say
In Derry of the little hills.

Francis Ledwidge
(1891-1917)

The Lark in the Clear Air

Dear thoughts are in my mind
And my soul soars enchanted,
As I hear the sweet lark sing
In the clear air of the day.
For a tender beaming smile
To my hope has been granted,
And tomorrow she shall hear
All my fond heart would say.

I shall tell her all my love,
All my soul's adoration;
And I think she will hear me
And will not say me nay.
It is this that fills my soul
With its joyous elation,
As I hear the sweet lark sing
In the clear air of the day.

Samuel Ferguson
(1810-1886)

THE MEETING OF THE WATERS

There is not in the wide world a valley so sweet
As that vale in whose bosom the bright waters meet;
Oh! the last rays of feeling and life must depart,
Ere the bloom of that valley shall fade from my heart.

Yet it *was* not that nature had shed o'er the scene
Her purest of crystal and brightest of green;
'Twas *not* her soft magic of streamlet and hill,
Oh! no, – it was something more exquisite still.

'Twas that friends, the belov'd of my bosom, were
    near,
Who made every dear scene of enchantment more
    dear,
And who felt how the best charms of Nature improve,
When we see them reflected from looks that we love.

Sweet vale of Avoca! how calm could I rest
In thy bosom of shade, with the friends I love best,
Where the storms that we feel in this cold world
    should cease,
And our hearts, like thy waters, be mingled in peace.

Thomas Moore
(1779-1852)

THE MOTHER

I do not grudge them: Lord, I do not grudge
My two strong sons that I have seen go out
To break their strength and die, they and a few,
In bloody protest for a glorious thing,
They shall be spoken of among their people,
The generations shall remember them,
And call them blessed;
But I will speak their names to my own heart
In the long nights;
The little names that were familiar once
Round my dead hearth.
Lord, thou art hard on mothers:
We suffer in their coming and their going;
And tho' I grudge them not, I weary, weary
Of the long sorrow – And yet I have my joy:
My sons were faithful, and they fought.

Padraig Pearse
(1879-1916)

ON AN ISLAND

You've plucked a curlew, drawn a hen,
Washed the shirts of seven men,
You've stuffed my pillow, stretched the sheet,
And filled the pan to wash your feet,
You've cooped the pullets, wound the clock,
And rinsed the young men's drinking crock;
And now we'll dance to jigs and reels,
Nailed boots chasing girls' naked heels,
Until your father'll start to snore,
And Jude, now you're married, will stretch on
    the floor.

J. M. Synge
(1871-1909)

Is it a Month

Is it a month since I and you
In the starlight of Glen Dubh
Stretched beneath a hazel bough
Kissed from ear and throat to brow,
Since your fingers, neck, and chin
Made the bars that fence me in,
Till Paradise seemed but a wreck
Near your bosom, brow, and neck
And stars grew wilder, growing wise,
In the splendour of your eyes!
Since the weasel wandered near
Whilst we kissed from ear to ear
And the wet and withered leaves
Blew about your cap and sleeves,
Till the moon sank tired through the ledge
Of the wet and windy hedge?
And we took the starry lane
Back to Dublin town again.

J. M. Synge
(1871-1909)

AN IRISH AIRMAN FORESEES HIS DEATH

I know that I shall meet my fate
Somewhere among the clouds above;
Those that I fight I do not hate,
Those that I guard I do not love;
My country is Kiltartan's Cross,
My countrymen Kiltartan's poor,
No likely end could bring them loss
Or leave them happier than before.

Nor law, nor duty bade me fight,
Nor public men, nor cheering crowds,
A lonely impulse of delight
Drove to this tumult in the clouds;
I balanced all, brought all to mind,
The years to come seemed waste of breath,
A waste of breath the years behind
In balance with this life, this death.

W. B. Yeats
(1865-1939)

IRELAND

I called you by sweet names by wood and linn,
You answered not because my voice was new,
And you were listening for the hounds of Finn
And the long hosts of Lugh.

And so, I came unto a windy height
And cried my sorrow, but you heard no wind,
For you were listening to small ships in flight,
And the wail on hills behind.

And then I left you, wandering the war
Armed with will, from distant goal to goal,
To find you at the last free as of yore,
Or die to save your soul.

And then you called to us from far and near
To bring your crown from out the deeps of time,
It is my grief your voice I couldn't hear
In such a distant clime.

Francis Ledwidge
(1891-1917)

First published in 1991 by
The Appletree Press Ltd,
19–21 Alfred Street, Belfast BT2 8DL
Tel: +44 232 243 074 Fax: +44 232 246 756
Copyright © 1991 The Appletree Press Ltd.
Printed in the E.C. All rights reserved.
No part of this publication may be reproduced
or transmitted in any form or by any means,
electronic or mechanical, photocopying,
recording or any information and retrieval
system, without permission in writing
from the publisher.

A Little Book of Irish Verse

First published in the United States in 1993
by Chronicle Books, 275 Fifth Street,
San Francisco, CA 94103

ISBN 0-8118-0508-5

Acknowledgements are due to the following for all
illustrations to the National Gallery of Ireland; for "The Old
Woman" by Joseph Campbell to Simon Campbell.

9 8 7 6 5 4 3 2 1